Date: 3/31/16

J 634.974 LEE
Lee, Jackie,
Coconut /

COCONUT

See It Grow

by Jackie Lee

Consultant: Karen C. Hall, PhD
Applied Ecologist, Botanical Research Institute of Texas
Fort Worth, Texas

BEARPORT
PUBLISHING

New York, New York

Credits

Title Page, © sunsetman/Shutterstock; TOC, © bdspn/iStock; 4, © julichka/iStock; 5T, © Marina Shanti/Shutterstock; 5M, © paulista/Shutterstock; 5B, © Viktor1/Shutterstock; 6–7, © Michal Durinik/Dreamstime; 8, © Wiro.Klyngz/Shutterstock; 9, © Ionut David/iStock; 10, © bdspn/iStock; 11, © O.Bellini/Shutterstock; 12L, © Niceregionpics/Dreamstime; 12R, © jakkapan/Shutterstock; 13, © temeekron/iStock; 14, © nojustice/iStock; 15, © orava/iStock; 16–17, © blickwinkel/Alamy; 18, © gopause/Shutterstock; 19, © NaamanAbreu/Shutterstock; 20, © Tim UR/Shutterstock; 21T, © Egor Rodynchenko/Shutterstock; 21B, © Butterfly Hunter/Shutterstock; 22L, © O.Bellini/Shutterstock; 22R, © Tryphosa Ho/Alamy; 23 (T to B), © Naaman Abreu/Shutterstock, © Egor Rodynchenko/Shutterstock, © Prapann/Shutterstock, © Tim UR/Shutterstock, and © Niceregionpics/Dreamstime; 24, © sunsetman/Shutterstock.

Publisher: Kenn Goin
Editorial Director: Natalie Lunis
Creative Director: Spencer Brinker
Design: Debrah Kaiser
Photo Researcher: Olympia Shannon

Library of Congress Cataloging-in-Publication Data

Lee, Jackie, active 2015, author.
  Coconut / by Jackie Lee.
      pages cm. — (See it grow)
  Includes bibliographical references and index.
  ISBN 978-1-62724-842-6 (library binding) — ISBN 1-62724-842-0 (library binding)
  1. Coconut—Juvenile literature. I. Title. II. Series: See it grow.
  SB401.C6L44 2016
  634.9'74—dc23
                                     2015008706

For more information, write to Bearport Publishing Company, Inc., 45 West 21st Street, Suite 3B, New York, New York 10010. Printed in the United States of America.

10 9 8 7 6 5 4 3 2 1

Contents

Coconut

Coconuts are used to make lots of tasty foods.

They are big, brown, and hairy.

How did they get that way?

Some people eat coconuts plain. Others use them to make soups, cookies, and drinks.

Coconuts grow on tall trees.

The trees are called coconut palms.

Coconut palms grow in warm places that get lots of rain.

7

A tall coconut palm grows from a seed.

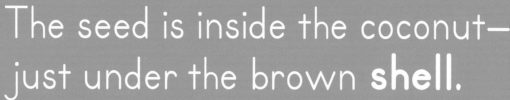

The seed is inside the coconut— just under the brown **shell.**

shell

husk

The outer part of a coconut is called the **husk**.

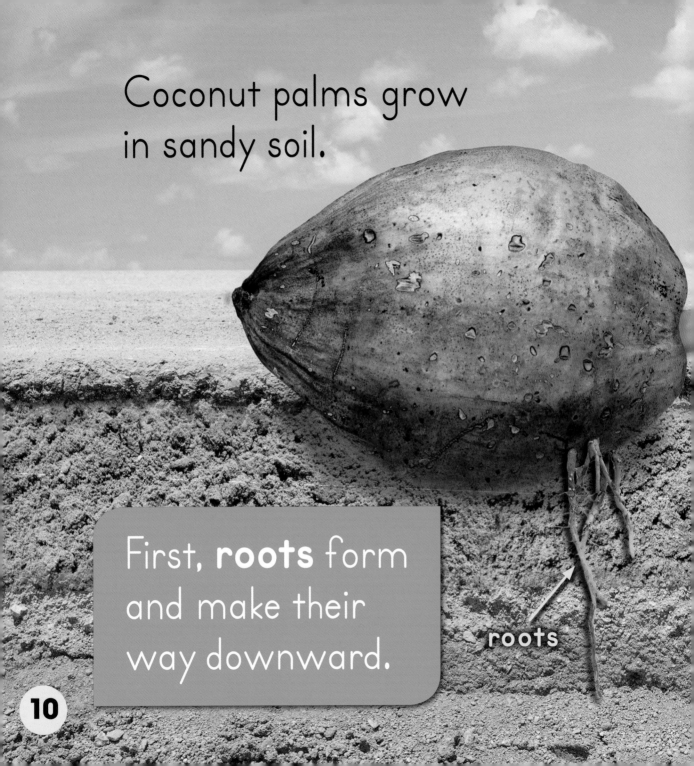

Coconut palms grow in sandy soil.

First, **roots** form and make their way downward.

roots

Later, a green **sprout** grows upward.

sprout

Every coconut has three dark spots called eyes. The sprout grows out of one of these spots.

The sprout keeps growing.

It becomes a young tree.

Leaves spread out
at the top of the tree.

The tree grows taller and taller.

A coconut tree can grow to be 100 feet (30.5 m) tall. That's as tall as a ten-story building.

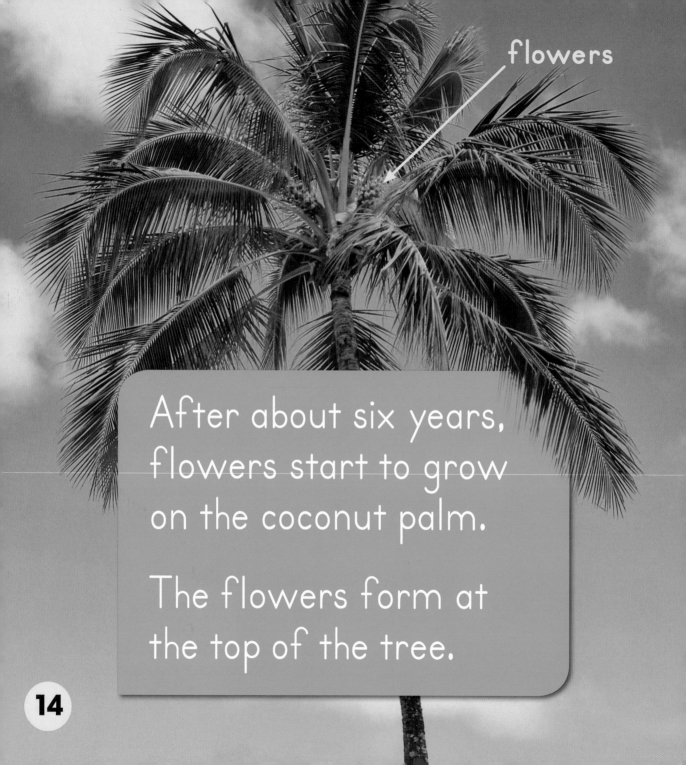

flowers

After about six years, flowers start to grow on the coconut palm.

The flowers form at the top of the tree.

The greenish-yellow
flowers grow on
long stems.

Some of the flowers form small round fruits.

These are baby coconuts!

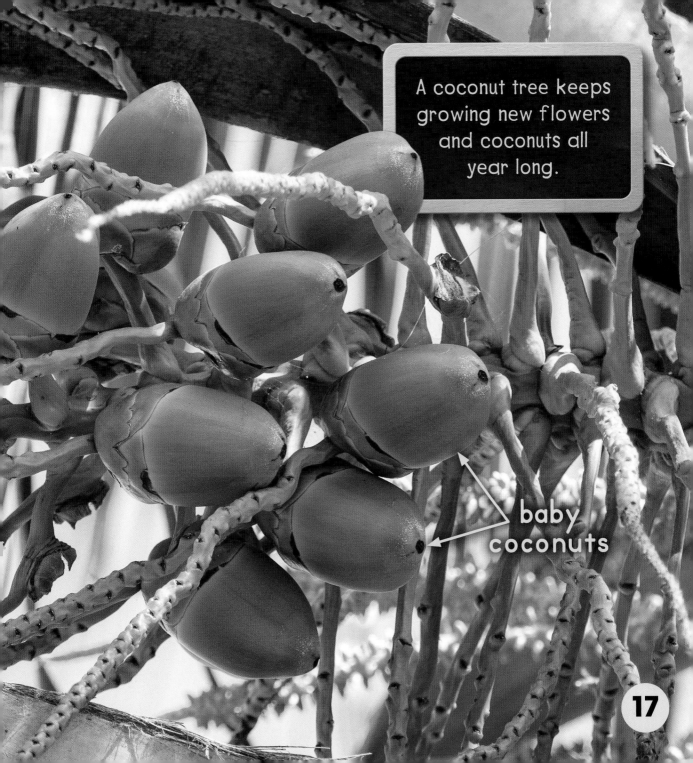

A coconut tree keeps growing new flowers and coconuts all year long.

baby coconuts

17

The fruits get bigger and bigger.

They change color, too.

At first, the husks are bright green. Over time, they turn yellow, orange, or brown.

Inside each husk is something round and brown.

Will it be eaten?

Or will it grow into
a new coconut palm?

The firm, white inside part
of the coconut is called the
meat. The meat is part of the
seed. It's also the part we eat.

meat

Coconut Facts

- The countries that grow the most coconuts are the Philippines, Indonesia, and India.

- A coconut seed is one of the biggest seeds in the world.

- It takes about a year for a coconut to grow and ripen.

- The word *coconut* comes from Portuguese and means "monkey face." People gave it that name because the three eyes together look like a face.

Glossary

 **husk** (HUSK) the smooth outer covering of a coconut

 **meat** (MEET) the firm, white inside part of a coconut

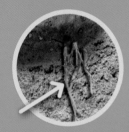 **roots** (ROOTS) parts of a plant that take in water and food from the soil

 **shell** (SHEL) the brown, hairy inner covering of a coconut

 **sprout** (SPROUT) a plant that has just started to grow

Index

Read More

Head, Honor. *Amazing Plants (Amazing Life Cycles).* Pleasantville, NY: Gareth Stevens (2008).

Lawrence, Ellen. *From Bird Poop to Wind: How Seeds Get Around (Plant-ology).* New York: Bearport (2013).

Learn More Online

To learn more about coconuts, visit
www.bearportpublishing.com/SeeItGrow

About the Author

Jackie Lee lives in upstate New York, where it is much too cold for coconut palms to grow.